PROGRESS
Not Perfection

A MEANINGFUL JOURNEY
WITH LASTING JOY

BY
Nancy Lynn
ROBERTS

oneseed PRESS

Progress Not Perfection
© 2013 by Nancy Lynn Roberts

Published by One Seed Press
7131 Riverside Parkway
Tulsa, OK 74136
918-933-5959

ISBN: 978-1-939250-02-5

Library of Congress Control Number: 2012920052

Printed in the United States of America

DEDICATION

I dedicate this book to my mother, Katie, who has always been perfect in God's eyes and will always be a work of progress towards excellence as well. I also dedicate this to the "village" of women my mother brought into my life, who helped her to raise me up in God's way: Aunt Suzanne Robbins, Aunt Nancy McGowan, Aunt Claudia Davidge, Aunt Judy Mayotte, Aunt Mary Kay Bullard, Aunt Francis Conerly, Aunt Jo Barton, Aunt Nan Buxton, Aunt Jan Hurley, Ferrelyn Oakes, and so many more!

CONTENTS

ACKNOWLEDGEMENTS

Without a circle of people who encouraged me, contributed to my writing, edited my work of the heart without piercing my heart and generally speaking gave to this book and to me their time, talents, and ministry, I would not have completed this journey! I offer extreme gratitude to the staff of One Seed Press and Insight International.

I want to first of all thank Tim McKitrick, D.Min., who encouraged me, prodded me, managed me, corrected me, helped me, and even motivated me along the way to never stop believing in the vision God put in my heart to write this book.

I also want to thank John Mason, an amazing Christian man, a best-selling author, and our friend, who forced me to dig deep and think hard about parts of my vision and to consider other possibilities for what I was saying or how I was saying it. His daughter Michelle Mason, who is on staff at Insight International, contributed to the process by educating me on all things necessary to publish a book for the first time. Without her, this book would never have been published and it certainly would not look the way it does.

To Jim Kochenburger, I express my deepest of gratitude for his editorial contributions and his willingness to challenge my writing, my thinking, and my word choice – all while helping me find how to make it better. He made what I wrote even better and together we might just be able to impact some people.

Finally, I want to thank my husband, Dan, and our children for allowing me the space and time so many early mornings to sit down in the quiet and write. Having this time together with God to express the things of my heart definitely gave me the strength and clarity during a time of healing from a broken heart so that I could become an even better mother, wife, and businesswoman.

INVITATION

Are you tired of hurting? Do you want to find joy, but always find pain? Are you exhausted trying to be the perfect Christian, perfect wife, perfect mother, perfect homemaker, and perfect employee/professional? If you are ready to stop the eternal search for perfection and start a meaningful journey of progress towards excellence, I invite you to join me!

Long ago, I let go of the "perfection" sticker and picked up a "work in progress" sticker that I wear openly. (Anyone who knows me well will tell you how flawed I really am!) I work hard at being an open book; as transparent about my weaknesses, mistakes, and failures as I am about my successes. Because of this, my eyes have been opened to learn new truths about myself and my faith constantly. I would not trade the journey for anything. My faith and my determination to overcome have kept me on the path to "ever improving." I have a long way to go on this journey, but I have traveled a long way from where I started. With each truth I discover and add to my life, I make a step of progress towards excellence.

It is my prayer that the seeds of truth God planted in me through many special people will become rooted in you through this book. May these truths kick-start your own journey on the pathway to progress. If your experience is like mine, you will be transformed in the process.

This book is designed to allow you to work through thirty godly truths in thirty days. One of the keys to your transformation will be the "Step to Progress" section of each day's reading. This section will ensure you make great progress as you write down in your own words how the truth of the day applies to your life. It also provides you with steps to follow that will help you make progress and actually see transformation in your life.

Whether you choose to go through this one-on-one with God or as part of a Bible study or small group, get started with these truths to find a new way to live, love, and enjoy each day of your life.

1
LIVE A LIFE OF LAUGHTER!

When I attended Wednesday Night Youth Club as a youth in Oklahoma City, our ministers drew us to church each week with zany, fun-filled activities, always followed by words of instruction from God. Each week, we arrived to find some new, crazy thing to do – whether we dressed in zany costumes, had a whipped cream fight, or tied balloons to our feet and tried to walk around without bouncing our balloons into one another – we were always doing something fun.

Those ministers and volunteers knew that the best way to attract others to God is to draw

THE BEST WAY TO ATTRACT OTHERS TO GOD IS TO DRAW THEM IN WITH THE LOVE AND LAUGHTER OF LIFE.

them in with the love and laughter of life. The joy of living the blessed and abundant life is far more intriguing than hearing about a book of rules. The safety of living, playing, and laughing within the lines of obedience God designed for us is far more attractive than the picture of what happens to our lives when we stray far afield from God. Remove the judgment, the criticism, the sharp jabs, and the spiteful humor. Find the things that make you laugh, love, and smile – share these things with others.

Laugh at yourself. Laugh with your friends and family. Laugh at the craziness in this world. Laugh at the mistakes you (and others) make. When you can laugh at these things, you will be in a place to do something about them. Refuse to create laughter with hurtful or derogatory comments or words. (Tearing others down will not build you up.) Instead, find the common thread of silliness that runs through us all.

When your spouse forgets to flush the toilet, smile and remember how often you have lost your keys or left your dirty clothes on the floor. When your child leaves the back door wide open and the dogs escape (again!), laugh and realize that you did the same thing when you were their age. Find joy in these moments and turn the anger or frustration into smiles and endearing love.

Use today to show the people in your life how you can laugh at yourself and your own life because you know who you are in Christ, who God is, what He has for you, and what He will do for you and anyone who follows Him.

> *"Our mouths were filled with laughter, our tongues with songs of joy." (Psalm 126:2)*

⋅⟨≡⊙≡⟩⋅

STEP TO PROGRESS

Take time today to write down things in your life that make you laugh. Share these with two other people so that they too can be full of "songs of joy."

_____

_____

_____

_____

_____

PROGRESS *Not Perfection*

2
LOOK AND SEE!

Each summer, my parents sent me to a beautiful camp nestled in the Colorado Rocky Mountains, near the base of Pikes Peak, just outside of Colorado Springs. The camp afforded this Oklahoma flatlander the opportunity to climb Pikes Peak, ride horses, camp out in the open air, and generally live in the great splendor God created.

Each Sunday, we held a prayer service high in the mountains. We were invited to pray and worship the God who made the beauty that surrounded us. I remember sitting on those rocks so many times, reveling in the glory of God's Kingdom. The mountains, the rocks, the valleys, the slopes, the views – it all amazed me. Even today, I love to climb those mountains and sit high on the rocks in awe of God's wonder, in realization of the vastness of His creation. In fact, I try to drive my children up to the mountains each year so that we can bask in the glory of God together.

GOD INVITES US TO SLOW DOWN THE PACE AND SET ASIDE A WINDOW OF TIME TO CONNECT WITH HIM.

As the business and the "busyness" of life take over, we often stop taking the time to revel in God's glory. We race from one event to the next with hardly a breath in between, hoping we do not miss something important or miss out on something "everyone else is doing." What does such a life bring, other than exhaustion, worry, or a sense of inferiority and insecurity?

God invites us to slow down the pace and set aside a window of time to connect with Him. Revel in the beauty of His Kingdom – not simply once each year when your family goes on a vacation – but each and every day, even moment by moment. Stop with your child to enjoy the little ladybug on the flower petal. Look at the leaves of grass and trees and realize how amazing it is that God made each of these. Slow down your pace enough to see the beauty of what is around you. Remember what Mother Teresa knew best, that none of us truly owns what is here on this earth, and the only thing we have to consider is the footprint we will leave when we are gone.

Take time to look around at the land, the sky, the hills, the wheat fields and trees, and thank God for all He created. When you spend time with God each day, it is much easier to focus on these things.

Dig into God's Word and follow it. Let it come alive within you. Allow it to shape and mold you into Christ's likeness. Find joy in taking that time away and notice how many more times throughout the day you stop and revel in the wonder of all that surrounds you. God's Kingdom is glorious. Rejoice in it! God's creation is beautiful and great. Praise Him for all that He has made.

> *"I lift up my eyes to the mountains – where does my help come from? My help comes from the Lord, the Maker of heaven and earth." (Psalm 121:1-2)*

STEP TO PROGRESS

Commit to set aside time each day to seek God's Word in your life – even if it is just ten minutes.

Consider rising a bit earlier, taking time in your car in the parking lot at work before walking in, or setting aside part of your lunchtime. Crack open God's book, turn to Psalms and start reveling in the Word of God. Wherever you are, bask in the splendor of what God has made. Repeat this every day for one week and write down what you see (that you otherwise would not have seen) as a result!

_____

_____

_____

_____

_____

_____

_____

_____

_____

_____

_____

_____

_____

_____

_____

3
GOD SEES IT ALL!

Do you remember when you first realized who God was – the all-knowing, ever-present, all-powerful Maker of heaven and earth – who watched over you and knew all there was to know about you (even the things that you yourself could not see)? This realization is life-changing. When you realize that God sees and knows everything, denial and hiding what is in your heart is no longer possible. After all, God sees it all!

This is a stopping point for many people who are on a pathway of getting to know God. Instead of simply resting in the fact that God sees all of us – the good, bad, and the ugly – we rebel. We push back against this truth and we throw the blanket of rebellion over it. We deny God's ability to see it all and we try to hide from the truth about ourselves.

We give power to our denial with excuses and lies. Are you stronger because of your rebellion or because of your ability to submit to the authority of God over your life?

Your Maker and Creator sees all, knows all, and is powerful over all. God is greater than anything in the world – He is greater than the darkness and His words alone created the light that shattered the darkness in the beginning of creation. He sees your rebellion, sees the denial, and hears the lies. God calls you to set all of those aside.

Are you living a transparent life while you shine the light of God, or are you hiding under a bush of denial and secrecy? Burn through that bush and be the fruitful vine – thorns and all – that God is calling you to be.

"He rules forever by his power, his eyes watch the nations – let not the rebellious rise up against him." (Psalm 66:7)

GOD SEES IT ALL!

STEP TO PROGRESS

Write down one area in your life where you are pushing back, digging in, or rebelling against God. Write down what you are going to do to overcome your rebellion with God's help. Tell someone you trust (that you know will hold you accountable), that you are going to overcome this in your life. Keep track in your calendar of how many days in a row you are successful at overcoming this issue until you know you have defeated it. Read God's Word each day for strength.

PROGRESS *Not Perfection*

4

FORGET ABOUT
WHAT YOU HAVE,
WEAR, OR DO

This life and the world teach us that the more we achieve the better we are. The larger the house we have, the more important we are. The higher up we go in an organization, the more significant we are as a person. The more money we make, the more valued our opinion is. The more important the people we know, the more important we are. The more expensive the social club, the more expensive the clothes, the larger the jewelry, the more important we are – the list goes on and on.

As early as age fourteen, I felt the impact of this world on my soul. I could never be as pretty or as perfect as the models in the magazines. I could never do everything perfectly God wanted me to do.

Like many other young people, I experienced a breakdown. Thank God for the wise counsel and example of godly women in my life – my Aunt Nancy, Aunt Claudia, Aunt Judy, Aunt Mary Kay, and others. Through their own lives they taught me that I was focused on the wrong things. Because of them, I came to believe that God loved me just the way I was and my aging body was just a part of this miracle called life. It was a breakthrough for me.

Don't get me wrong; this is an area of challenge I still face as time goes on. Each new wrinkle, sag line, or physical limitation presents me with a hurdle to overcome, based in worldly physical images of beauty. With God's help, I make progress in this every day, every year, and every decade. I focus not on losing weight but on gaining health. I strive not to go on a diet but to eat food that will fuel me. I seek not to have the perfect figure but to be physically fit and strong so that I can do all that God has called me to do. I may not be perfect (I love cookies and ice cream!), but I do keep a healthy balance when it comes to physical fitness. The same holds true for my spirit and my mind.

God teaches us something very different from the idea of worldly perfection that society projects. He teaches us that He loves us no matter how we look, whom we know, what position we hold, how much money we make, or what we have or have

GOD KNOWS WE ARE NOT PERFECT AND HE LOVES US ANYWAY.

not achieved. God knows we are not perfect and He loves us anyway. He loves to see us progress toward the perfection He has set before us. He wants us to grow continually in our knowledge and understanding of His love, His way of life, and His purpose for our lives. He is far less critical and far more loving and inviting than we might imagine. His methods of correction are expressions of His loving-kindness.

To shift your focus from worldly value to godly value, you will have to turn off the messages of this world. Throw away the Hollywood-focused magazines, turn off the gossip channels, and shut down the advertisements designed to convince you that without their product, you are nothing. Pick up God's book and read just how valuable and loved you are. Then read about the life God wants for you and start focusing on how you can start living the life of peace, joy, and love. It is your progress not your perfection that God rewards.

> *"Do not conform any longer to the pattern of this world, but be transformed by the renewing of your mind. Then you will be able to test and approve what God's will is – his good, pleasing and perfect will." (Romans 12:2)*

STEP TO PROGRESS

To what sources do you turn when you are stressed and tired? Excited and joyful? What spiritual food are you ingesting on a daily basis? The TV? A newspaper? A magazine? Texting on your cell phone or messaging friends? How do you start your day? On Facebook? Reading news? Checking messages? Write down all the places in a typical day where you seek spiritual nourishment.

Make a commitment for one week to start each day by getting nourishment from God's Word. Pull out and read God's Word, your favorite devotional, or a Christian fiction book. Listen to a Christian teaching CD instead of watching a reality TV show. Make a seven-day commitment to seek a source based on God's Word. Write down the difference it makes.

Expand your commitment from one week to one month. Before you know it, you will find a new you. God's Word will transform not only your mind but your heart. He will get your day started right, will help you in the middle of it by keeping you on track, and will tuck you into bed peacefully. You will slowly begin to become all that God meant you to be. Remember…progress is a process. Start moving in the direction God wants for you. Before you know it, God's beauty will be in you and will be shining through!

PROGRESS *Not Perfection*

5
JUST ASK

One day, I found myself in a life situation that made it clear I had fallen away from God's will for me. I had made choices that landed me in a bad place. I was broken and living a life that was all about money. I did not have a clue how to solve the problems, but I knew that with God's help, I might be able to start making a new life for myself. I began my journey by falling to my knees next to my bed and saying aloud, "God, please help! Everything I have is Yours and everything I do will be for You."

That night, before I fell asleep, I began what became a nightly habit of reading a devotional book, looking back over my day, then writing down where I had gone astray from God's Word in my home, with my family, with my neighbors or friends, and with my co-laborers. I wrote down the ways that I had not lived up to the life God wanted for me and asked, in writing, for God's forgiveness and strength to walk uprightly the next day. Then I did something very important – I received His forgiveness and gained His assurance that He would give me what I needed to overcome all obstacles I would face the next day. This became a truly transformative nightly habit. I miss a few days here and there, but I have never given up the practice of spending my last waking moments talking to God.

As I do this each evening, I have to fully acknowledge and accept my brokenness and my failures. Only then am I ready to receive His gift of forgiveness and start down the path of healing and wholeness. I have found that as I walk down this path of healing, I am more ready to love God, myself, and others. It stops me from criticizing, judging, or condemning others for their brokenness because I see my own brokenness each day. As you continue to seek forgiveness for your own brokenness and love

AS YOU SEEK FORGIVENESS, YOU WILL FIND STRENGTH IN YOUR WEAKNESS AND LOVE IN YOUR FAILURES.

others in their brokenness, you will find strength in your weakness and love in your failures. All you have to do is ask – and then receive what God has to offer.

"Until now you have not asked for anything in my name. Ask and you will receive, and your joy will be complete." (John 16:24)

⊱──═══◉═══──⊰

STEP TO PROGRESS

As you think back on your life, write down the worst things you have done, the worst choices you have made, the most harmful things you have said, and the most pain you have caused others. Now take that and turn it into a heartfelt prayer. Just as I did, fall down on your knees in fear and humility, and ask your Father God to forgive you for your brokenness and failure. Jesus tore down the veil of hidden shame when He died on the cross. Ask God, in the name of His Son, to forgive you and put you back together again.

PROGRESS *Not Perfection*

6

IT MATTERS WHO
IS WITH YOU

In my college years and even into my twenties, I turned my attention to many things that were not of God. Oh, the mistakes I made – the choices I wish I could undo! I sought love in all the wrong places and ways. I let go of dreams God had put inside me.

Through it all, God always put people in my life who, like me, knew Him and loved Him. God intentionally put men and women in my life to keep me headed in the right direction, to deepen my walk, to steer me back, and to show me a different path when I veered astray from His Word and ways. God drew me

GOD DREW ME BACK TO HIMSELF WITH PEOPLE – IMPERFECT, GOD-FEARING, GOD-FOLLOWING PEOPLE.

back to Himself with people – imperfect, but God-fearing, God-following people.

Unfortunately, the reverse has also been true. I can look back over my life and see people I followed down a path to disaster. They were seeking pleasure, things, or status more than they were seeking God, love, or truth. The result was a lot of choices I regret and circumstances I wish I had not helped to create. I always had to pay a price for following those people, and I have typically learned a great lesson from each in the process. It was never pretty, joyful, or peaceful on that path, but I have always steered my way back to God's path for my life.

Look around at the people in your life. Are you surrounded by people who are seeking and following God? Regardless of whether they are perfect or not, are they drawing you toward God or away from Him? What kind of person are you to others? Are you planting seeds of truth or seeds of destruction?

"Don't you know that you yourselves are God's temple and that God's Spirit dwells in your midst?" (1 Corinthians 3:16)

STEP TO PROGRESS

Write down the names of all the people God has put in your life that keep you going in the right direction. What are some things they have done to help you stay on track or get you back on track when you were headed in the wrong direction? Take time to thank them for what they have done for you! Write a note, send an e-mail, message them, or thank them in person. Now go out and help someone else get headed back in God's direction, just as these people did for you.

_____

_____

_____

_____

_____

_____

_____

_____

_____

_____

PROGRESS *Not Perfection*

7
ANSWER THE CALL

I remember trying to decide what was next for my life after graduating from college in California. I had the world at my fingertips – internship experience with Jet Propulsion Laboratories, an opportunity to attend UCLA for graduate school, and an amazing college undergraduate degree in cognitive sciences from Pomona College (an independent study program consisting of a three-department major in robotics, statistics, and cognitive psychology). Where did I end up going for my post-graduate studies? The University of Oklahoma, College of Law.

The world may well look at my chosen path and ask, "What happened? What was wrong with you when you made that decision?" But when I look at my path, I see something completely different. God called me to go back to where my family was. He called me to not live a life separate and apart from those He had first given to me. When God calls us and we listen, He reveals His plans. Today, I am running a technology-based company that is highly regulated and that relies on programming, cognitive psychology, and statistics! We use the past to try to predict the future and assess people to determine if they are a good fit for specific positions within companies. I could never have anticipated how all those different studies would come together – but God did!

When we follow God's call, we sometimes cannot see far ahead into the future. What we cannot see is a part of what God has planned. If we are following God's plan, we end up living out His will for our lives.

> *"If you fully obey the LORD your God and care-fully follow all his commands I give you today, the LORD your God will set you high above all the nations on earth." (Deuteronomy 28:1)*

STEP TO PROGRESS

- What plans does God want to reveal to you?

- Have you stopped to listen to Him instead of just listening to what the world is telling you?

- Are you following the direction of God's call, or are you headed where the world wants you to go?

- Which direction is God calling you, and are you willing to follow?

What you build up and store on this earth will wither away – but what you do for God will have everlasting impact. Write down the direction God is calling you to go and what you are doing to follow God's plan for your life.

PROGRESS *Not Perfection*

8

GOD IS YOUR "DO-OVER" BUTTON

Have you ever just fallen to your knees and wished you could press a magic "do-over" button? Have you ever made a choice that took you down a path that changed your life forever? I have.

The good news is when we make wrong choices, God does not leave us. God follows us wherever we go, no matter what. More importantly, He loves us through it all. God's love is limitless. When we make mistakes, He

GOD FOLLOWS US WHEREVER WE GO. NO MATTER WHAT.

is waiting for us to fall to our knees and pray, to reverse course from whatever choice took us in the wrong direction, to acknowledge our mistakes to others, and then start down a new path with a renewed sense of godly purpose and determination. God's favor will shine down upon us as we walk in obedience to His Word.

When you find yourself in that place – wishing you could just rewind the tape and push a "do-over" button, fall to your knees and pray. Tell God how sorry you are that you made the choice you made and ask Him to lead you to where He wants you to go. God will give you the power and strength to make it through the mess you have created. He will hold your hand and carry you as you cross over the woods and onto the path He had originally laid down for your travels.

In the process, He will show you His love in strangers you meet, words that are said, and moments that are realized. In the end, He will have strengthened you and made your foundation firm.

> *"But at the evening offering I arose from my humiliation, even with my garment and my robe torn, and I fell on my knees and stretched out my hands to the LORD my God."*
> (Ezra 9:5 NASB)

STEP TO PROG

What are the choices or evei   .... ior which you most wish you could have a "do-over"? Write them here. Then fall to your knees and pray. Pray for God's forgiveness, guidance, and love. Receive these things from Him and lay aside those wrong choices and events. Let God have them. He may not let you do them over, but He will let you start to "do differently" immediately. What are you going to do differently starting today? Write it down and pray for God's strength as you enter this new phase of doing and living.

_____

_____

_____

_____

_____

_____

_____

_____

_____

_____

9

IDENTIFY YOUR "ANGELS"

There I was, at the foot of my beautiful bed in my picture-perfect home, praying to God and giving Him my entire life – career and all. I had detoured from the life He had for me and I had no idea how to change the course of things. What I did know was that I was there because of my own choices not to follow the Word and will of God for my life. I also knew I was miserable. The next day, a gift from God appeared in the form of a married woman who lived a block away. She was looking for a partner to go on early morning walks with her.

BEFORE YOU KNOW IT, GOD MAY SEND AN "ANGEL" INTO YOUR LIFE.

When you call on God to see you through a rough patch in

your life, be prepared. Before you know it, God may send an "angel" into your life. Many times, God has intervened in my life in the form of people who walked with me during a time of turmoil, in the form of a stranger who spoke a word to me that answered the prayer of my heart, in the form of a gift received anonymously in the mail, and many more.

God sends people into our lives and speaks to us through them. So when you look to God for help, be on the lookout for these messengers from God. Listen for them, watch for them, and pay attention to what they say. They are more than just people walking by. They are messengers from a God who loves you enough to give you what you need or tell you what you need to hear (even if it is not what you want to hear).

For nearly three years, my God-given walking partner and I walked and talked. She shared her faith and it slowly infiltrated my way of thinking and changed my heart. I grew strong in the Word of God as I started reading and learning more of it. That "angel" turned my life around. Instead of heading in the wrong direction, I started heading in the direction God intended for me in the first place.

At other times, God blessed me and worked through my life, allowing me to play the role of God's messenger who reached out and touched a stranger with His love. Thank God for the people He puts in our lives.

> *"Do not forget to show hospitality to strangers, for by so doing some people have shown hospitality to angels without knowing it." (Hebrews 13:2)*

STEP TO PROGRESS

Who are the "angels" God has put in your life? Write down their names and thank God for them. Are you remembering to allow God to work through you so that you can be used for God's purposes in the life of someone else? Who is God touching through you? Write down the names of these individuals and ask God to continue to use you. When you do these two things – both recognize God's "angels" and realize that you can be one

of them – you will fully live out God's purpose for
your life.

10
SPEAK WHAT YOU CANNOT YET SEE

Have you ever known someone who glimpsed just beneath the surface of who you were to see the person that you had the potential to become – even though you were not yet that person on the outside? Perhaps it was a favorite teacher of yours; the one who made you feel more special than anyone else, who believed in you when even you did not believe in you. All children need an adult in their life who does this for them. If we were truly honest with ourselves, most of us adults need this too. Everyone has the opportunity to be that perceptive and encouraging person to those around them!

Each day I try to think how I can become better at drawing out the beauty in others. I have come a long way in this, but I have a long way to go! Thank goodness God is looking at my progress and not at my perfection! God has impressed me over the past five years with the importance of really listening to others instead of just being on a mission to get done what I want done. He has spoken to me about seeing what lies inside of someone and then helping them to see it too. I have spoken out loud the potential that someone has rather than the reality of where they are.

The truth is, this is how God calls us to live with one another – acting on faith that God made each of us to be something beautiful, but recognizing that we all need a little help to blossom. We are called to walk through life seeing and speaking out loud the beauty inside of the people around us, and to then give them the water and fertilizer they need to come to life and bloom on the outside. Start speaking to the people around you as if they are already what God is calling them to be. Start speaking to yourself as if you are already what God is calling you to be. Then watch what happens. They (and you) will begin to realize all you are speaking!

SPEAK OUT LOUD THE BEAUTY...

"As it is written: 'I have made you a father of many nations.' He is our father in the sight of God, in whom he believed – the God who gives life to the dead and calls into being things that were not." (Romans 4:17)

STEP TO PROGRESS

Identify one person in your life today in whom you see God-given beauty and potential. What can you do, starting today, to help water and fertilize that beauty and potential, causing them to bloom on the outside of that person? Continually tell the person who God is calling them to become. Watch the impact of your words on his or her face and write down their response and reaction. Continue this for at least a month and document the changes you see in this person throughout this time. Thank God for the beauty that blooms as a result!

PROGRESS *Not Perfection*

11
"AND THE GREATEST OF THESE IS LOVE"

From our earliest age, we are bombarded with worldly messages of what love is supposed to look like: it looks like a Walt Disney fairy tale, with birds singing and princess dresses flowing. It looks like your spouse bringing home roses, "just because." It looks like diamond earrings on your anniversary. It looks like a heart-shaped bed on your wedding night. These images are designed to evoke an emotion that we begin to associate with the word "love."

The truth is that love is a life-long choice to act, not just to feel. It is a choice we make every day, despite how bad our circum- stances may be, regardless of how

THE TRUTH IS THAT LOVE IS A LIFELONG CHOICE TO ACT, NOT JUST TO FEEL.

many wrong choices someone else has made, irrespective of how unlovable someone is. Real love does not always feel great when one chooses it, but the investment in it as a choice will result in relationships that ultimately blossom into the love of the fairy tales.

True love is not a feeling, but a repeated series of decisions coupled with actions. We choose to hug our toddler instead of scream when they throw the glass dish across the room (and look up to see how we will react). We choose to hug our teenager when they come home to announce that they wrecked the new car we just purchased for them. We choose to hug our spouse when they come home grumpy and irritable from a long day at the office. In these moments, our first "feeling" may not be love, but we make the choice to put feelings and emotions aside and to do what God is calling us to do – to love anyway.

So, as you go about your day today, ask yourself: *To whom can I show true love? Who can I make the active choice to love; regardless of what they are doing, what others are saying about them (or me), and without consideration of how lovable they are?* This is the kind of love God wants us to give and receive from others (and to receive from Him). Don't miss out on it! Remember, "the greatest of these is love" (1 Corinthians 13:13).

> *"My command is this: Love each other as I have loved you." (John 15:12)*

STEP TO PROGRESS

Work to choose love today in all circumstances. Take time to write down each instance when you made a choice to respond to someone with emotions or feelings rather than love. Identify the emotion or feeling you first had and what you did to override that with the choice to love. Love simply acts regardless of how it feels. Write down the acts of love you chose today.

_____

_____

_____

_____

PROGRESS *Not Perfection*

12

ENJOY WHAT YOU ARE GIVEN, BUT KNOW WHAT LASTS

As a parent, I sometimes wonder if I am planting the right things in my children. I grew up in a family that focused on three things: living out our faith, loving others, and getting a great education. Different seasons of my life have caused me to focus on growing in different areas. My early years touched on learning and growing in all of these areas, but much of my time was spent in school.

From there, it seemed that I needed to put my education to work in the world. So once I had achieved my degrees, I went to work to excel in my career. My husband and I worked fifty to seventy hours a week for nearly twenty years! To some, this may have seemed crazy, but if you watched closely what we were doing during those long days and longer weeks, you would see we were oftentimes using our time to touch the lives of others – long conversations with people who were hurting, coaching sessions designed to encourage or grow people, putting in the work it takes to improve the way people or our companies were doing things. Early in our married life, we decided that while we wanted to excel at whatever God put in our lives, we would lay down in an instant whatever we were doing to follow what God called us to do.

I did not just go to the grocery store, for instance; I visited with the single mom in line who looked like she was having a rough day. We invited children into our home and spent time with them. We brought a child from a broken home into our lives. We spent time talking to a drunk, single man who had lived a life lost in pain. We received no awards, public recognition, or plaques on the wall for these extra activities. Many times, even the people closest to us did not see all that we were doing, but this is how we chose to spend our time.

We found that when we ignored God's call to take time out for others, we suffered. When we responded immediately to God's call, we experienced times of great joy. We had to learn to make the most of the opportunities God gave us and focus our hearts on what really lasts.

WE HAD TO LEARN TO FOCUS OUR HEARTS ON WHAT REALLY LASTS.

Some question the wisdom of our determination to combine vocational excellence with obedience to God (the world says "time is money and money is wasted on others!"); but for us, it has been more about laying down our lives and possessions to pursue God's purposes (sometimes giving to those who do not deserve it, giving people a chance when nobody else would do that, or even pursuing something for the sake of establishing the truth with the hope that it would turn a person towards God) rather than our own. Jim Elliot has said, "He is no fool who gives what he cannot keep to gain what he cannot lose."

> *"I have seen all the things that are done under the sun; all of them are meaningless, a chasing after the wind." (Ecclesiastes 1:14)*

STEP TO PROGRESS

Take time to explore these thoughts and questions as you consider whether you are enjoying what you have been given and whether you are living as if you know what lasts.

When you look at your life, are you chasing after a title, career, position, making a name for yourself, membership in an elite club, or social status? Or, are you spending your time chasing after a meaningful relationship with God? Why?

Are you investing in what you cannot lose (heavenly treasure) or what you cannot keep (earthly wealth and position)? Why do you say this?

When you catch what you are chasing, what will be left in your arms? Is it something that equates to a plaque on a wall? Or, is it a life full of lives you have touched and hearts you have helped to change? Explain.

When you have chased after the things of this world, have you been fulfilled to the fullest?

What one thing are you chasing after right now that you are ready to lay down so that you can chase after God more fully?

PROGRESS *Not Perfection*

13

ARE YOU HUNGRY?

When was the last time you were hungry? I mean really hungry, not just, *Oh, I wish I had a root beer float and cheeseburger right now* kind of hungry. I am talking about being so hungry that your insides hurt, you are weak in every part of your body, you are not sure if you can see clearly, and you have no strength to cry. Most of us do not really know what it means to be really physically hungry – we just have a sliver of an idea of what it must be like.

When it comes to spiritual hunger, however, the world is full of starving people! So many of us are walking through life in this condition. We are starving and hungry for God's Word, spiritually void of the love that God wants us to have in our hearts, dependent on emotional and physical swings, desires, and needs. We work to the point of exhaustion. We move so fast we have lost focus. We are self-absorbed to the point of being blind to the needs of others, and walking around wounded while we inflict pain on others. Does this sound like a place you are or have been? Most of us have been there at some point and we are surrounded by people who are still there.

If you are in that place today or want to keep from going there, try something new. Start your day going to God's Word and get your daily spiritual food. His Word is the food that gives us what we need to navigate through the hurts and trials of this world.

IF YOU EAT THE RIGHT SPIRITUAL FOOD, YOU WILL FIND RENEWAL, STRENGTH, HEALING, AND HOPE.

If you eat the right spiritual food each day, you will find renewal and strength, healing and hope, redirection and correction. You will find just what you need to face the challenges each day brings. Open your heart and listen. Do not be afraid. He will draw you to a place of peace that carries you through your trials. He will lead you away from temptation and remind you how to live a life of love. He will refill your spiritual tank each day so you have the fuel you need!

Fill your spiritual stomach each day with God's Word. Then go out and be all God wants you to be.

"Give us each day our daily bread." (Luke 11:3)

STEP TO PROGRESS

Identify a portion of the beginning of your day you can set aside to spend even just fifteen minutes in God's Word. It could be right when you wake up, or just before you walk into work. Pick one book of the Bible to read from beginning to end during this time. Commit to one chapter each day.

Psalms is a great place to start. Follow it up with Proverbs. Then move to the New Testament and do a comparison of the first five books (Matthew, Mark, Luke, John, and Acts). Follow that with a study of the life and teachings of Paul. Go back to the days of Moses to gain a historical perspective. You may want to consider reading through a *One*

Year Bible. These provide a reading plan of chapters and verses to read each day so that you can read through the whole Bible in one year. No matter which of these you choose to do, make a commitment to spend time each day reading and meditating on God's Word, the Bible.

14

BE ON ALERT

Everywhere you look, doorways to disaster surround you. Whether it be the gossip magazine on the grocery store rack, the wine glass or bar calling out to you after a difficult day, the friends who get together every month for a "night out," the person who flaunts all the beautiful things they have that you don't, or that handsome guy or beautiful woman at the office. All of these things have one thing in common: If you allow your heart, mind, and soul to say yes to them, you can rapidly find yourself walking down a path that leads you away from following one or more of God's commands.

WE CARRY A NEW RESPONSIBILITY: TO BE ON ALERT FOR THESE "DOORWAYS TO DISASTER."

When we make the choice to follow God and accept Jesus as

our Lord and Savior, something changes. We carry a new responsibility: to be on alert for these "doorways to disaster." We have to keep our eyes and ears open, our hearts aware, and our spirits on guard for any door that opens and leads to what could be a disastrous choice. As I look back on my life, the times when I said yes to these kinds of things were the times when I went astray. Likewise, the times when I made the choice to say, "No thank you, God has something better for me to do right now," I found peace, knowing that I had done exactly what God was calling me to do.

So be on guard. Watch out! Beware. Only go through doorways that lead to those things that God says lead to life everlasting.

"Be on guard. Stand firm in the faith. Be courageous. Be strong." (1 Corinthians 16:13 NLT)

STEP TO PROGRESS

- Which doorways to disaster have you been able to avoid in the past? How were you able to do this?

- Which doorways to disaster have you opened and entered? Why?

- Which doorways are you keeping closed due to your focus on something else?

- When you look at the doorways in life you are walking through right now, do they lead you to do what God has called you to do? How?

Make a commitment to God to close the doorways to disaster and to open the doors to life everlasting He has cracked open for you.

PROGRESS *Not Perfection*

15
CHOOSE GOD'S SIDE

Have you ever played a sport? If you have, you understand that the team depends on each player being the best he or she can be at all times. You have to prepare, practice, and commit to not quit and stick it out even when the going gets tough. When you make a mistake, you have to learn what you did wrong and then keep practicing until you get it right. When game time comes, you have to walk out on the field or court and give it everything you have to win – you literally choose to do whatever it takes.

Our faith walk is no different. We must prepare every day and practice living the abundant life God wants for us. When we make a mistake, we must realize it, understand what we did wrong, and go at it again until we get it right. We must remember the little things make a big difference to God – how we treat our next-door neighbor, or how we respond to a stranger who asks for a dollar. When it comes to making big life decisions, we also have to know what God wants for us, choose to live according to His Word, and give Him everything we have.

ARE YOU READY TO APPROACH YOUR FAITH LIFE WITH THE SAME LEVEL OF DETERMINATION?

Are you ready to approach your faith life with the same level of determination and tenacity you use when arguing a point, playing a sport, winning a match, or making a business deal? Choose God's side now and give Him all that you are and all that you have. You will never regret it.

"Put on all of God's armor so that you will be able to stand firm against all strategies of the devil." (Ephesians 6:11 NLT)

<>=<>

STEP TO PROGRESS

Write down three things that you can add to your day today to "put on the armor of God," recognizing it will help you win the battle for your life. Some ideas could be: reading God's Word, speaking God's Word over your life, praising God for all He has done in your life, praying to God throughout the day in response to things that happen, eliminating words and actions that are not righteous in God's eyes, praying for an enemy, extending grace to someone who makes a mistake, giving love to someone who is otherwise unlovable, and more. These are the game rules for those who desire to live their lives following Jesus. Which of these things can you add to your day and life?

PROGRESS *Not Perfection*

16

ACHIEVEMENT VERSUS FULFILLMENT

To live in the world today, you must learn what it takes to achieve. Hard work, discipline, determination, drive, goal-setting, commitment – these are all common characteristics of any person who is viewed as an "achiever" in this life. We start instilling these traits in our children from an early age, rewarding them for every little worldly achievement: kindergarten graduations, honor rolls, soccer championships, gymnastics meets, choir contests, dance recitals, and more.

When the world sees you strive for perfection or to accomplish lofty goals, you risk being labeled an "overachiever," and it turns out, it could make you a poster child for a miserable existence. Alexandra

Robbins spent nearly two years traveling with and interviewing young students who qualified as over-achievers. She even wrote a book about them, *Overachievers*. They were straight-A students with high academic achievement scores, all-star athletes, accomplished artists or musicians – the list goes on. Most of these students had achieved more in their short eighteen years than most people will achieve in a lifetime.

Surprisingly, in nearly every interview Ms. Robbins conducted, these young people shared very similar ideas about how they felt about themselves and viewed their lives…they were uniformly miser-able. "Contemplating suicide," "Want to run away," "I am starving myself," and "Never good enough," are just a few poignant excerpts from their inter-views. Overachievement controlled their lives and they were exhausted as a result. These young people are worldly proof that "achievement brings fulfill-ment" is counter to truth – and it is directly counter to the Word of God.

Ecclesiastes 1 and 2 speak volumes of the empty life that results when one focuses on achievement.

Achievement Versus Fulfillment

It is only when we focus on meaningful living, the fulfillment of God's purpose for our own lives that we truly begin to "achieve." Fulfillment leads to achievement, not the other way around.

What do you spend your time doing? Are you focused on toiling or are you focused on fulfillment? Are you racking up achievements for your resume or are you fulfilling your purpose? Let go and let God do the work in your life, focusing your eyes, your heart, and your time on Him. What you will achieve as a result is an inner peace and a confident "knowing" that your life has true meaning and purpose.

ARE YOU RACKING UP ACHIEVEMENTS FOR YOUR RESUME OR FULFILLING YOUR PURPOSE?

> *"Yet when I surveyed all that my hands had done and what I had toiled to achieve, everything was meaningless, a chasing after the wind; nothing was gained under the sun."* (Ecclesiastes 2:11)

STEP TO PROGRESS

Write down the worldly achievements you have attained throughout your life. Now write down the ways in which you are fulfilling God's purpose for your life. Highlight in yellow your priorities in terms of time, money, or attention. Using a different color highlighter, highlight the ones you intend to make the focus of your time, money, or attention. Using the list you just developed, write out a vision statement for your life, along with a mission statement and a list of your core values. Post it where you will see it regularly: on your bathroom mirror or wall and on your desk. As you start each day, ask yourself how you will stay true to your vision statement that day and seek God's help to do so.

17
LIVE IT OUT LOUD

It is hard to believe that I was well into my mid-thirties before I did a full-blown study on what it means to abide in Christ and live the abundant life (John 10:10). Thank God for two women – Julie and Jolie – who introduced me to these keys to growth in my Christian walk! I look back and wonder how in the world I lived thirty-plus years as a Christian without having studied these key principles of what God wanted for me (and you) in this life. If this is something you have not studied, stop everything and do it now! It will change how you spend your time, where you focus your heart, and how your circumstances impact you.

An understanding of vines and tending a rose garden are both key to understanding the Bible verse from John 15:4 and what it takes to live out our faith. Just as a rose garden must be constantly tended, so must we study God's Word constantly. By doing so, we lower the risk of being hurt deeply by ugly, painful thorns. By pruning our dead branches (which every vine has), we make way for new life. By diligently feeding and watering, we can look forward to beautiful blossoms to bloom. The result of such planting, feeding, and pruning is a life lived on earth that smells as sweet as a rose.

THE RESULT OF SUCH PLANTING, FEEDING, AND PRUNING IS A LIFE THAT SMELLS AS SWEET AS A ROSE.

The key is to feed each day on the vitamin-packed words God has given us in the Bible. This is the way we learn to live the abiding, abundant life. Bathe your days in prayer to God and allow the Holy Spirit to live in and through you. Learn how to discern the difference between your own desires and God's desires for your life. If you spend time with God and read about Jesus' walk through life, you will begin to understand the life God is calling you to live. Stop focusing on making a rose and start focusing on doing what it takes to care for the vine and abide in it to live an abundant life. Only then will you start to grow.

> *"Abide in me, and I in you. As the branch cannot bear fruit by itself, unless it abides in the vine, neither can you, unless you abide in me."* (John 15:4 ESV)

STEP TO PROGRESS

When a vinedresser walks into a vineyard that has been neglected, the first thing he or she does is clear away the weeds and start to prune back the vines. When you look at your faith life, what do you need to clear out of your day and cut away so that you can grow in some new ways? Until the dead junk is cleared out, you will have no room for new life. Identify one area for pruning in your life today. Now make a commitment to God to cut out and throw away that part of your life so that you have room for God to grow something new in and through you.

PROGRESS *Not Perfection*

18
CHOOSE YOUR TEAM WISELY

Who are you? Who are you becoming? The first step to answering both of these questions is to look closely at those who surround you – those who are closest to you. Jeanne Mayo has a saying: "Show me your friends and I'll show you your future." With whom do you spend the most time? Who speaks into your life? Who do you trust? Are you surrounded by leaders or surrounded by complainers? Are you surrounded by instigators of bad stuff or instigators of positive change? Are you surrounded by people who are making the kind of choices you know you should make or by those who are making the kind of choices you know you shouldn't make (and would want to keep secret from the world)?

At one point in my life, I took a good look around and realized I was spending most of my time with people who were busy complaining. They were tired of their spouses, sick of politics, disgusted with the family down the street, wishing they had more or looked better – on and on it went. Worst of all, I saw that I was rapidly becoming like them! Instead of being surrounded by people who got up and made a difference, I was surrounded by people who got up to watch and talk about what other people were doing wrong! Have you been there?

So how do you go about surrounding yourself with a new team? First, you take a careful look at your calendar and make some drastic changes in where you go, what you do, and with whom you spend time. In our business life, we call this "looking at who is on the bus and making some stops to get the wrong ones off." If you are into investments, think of it like this – you invest in people who are sure to give a positive return on your investment.

My first step to changing those who surrounded me was to make some changes to...me. I stopped going to the "Mom's Night Out" events. I stopped trying to wear clothes that were meant for someone half my age. I stopped talking about what I did not like about my life. I started attending and then leading a Bible study. I started working on speaking aloud the awesome things I saw in my spouse and children (instead of only talking about their utter failures that drove me nuts). I started inviting people into my life who looked different from me and lived out their faith better than me.

If you are surrounding yourself with people who are focused on how to climb the social ladder, then that is who you will become. If you are surrounded by people who are committed to changing the world for the better, you too will start being a world-changer. If you surround yourself with people who spend their time criticizing others, you too will be critical of others. If you surround yourself with those who encourage and uplift others, you will do the same. The question for you is which team surrounds you?

IF YOU ARE SURROUNDED BY PEOPLE CHANGING THE WORLD, YOU TOO WILL BE A WORLD-CHANGER.

"As iron sharpens iron, so one person sharpens another." (Proverbs 27:17)

STEP TO PROGRESS

Write down the names of the people in whom you are investing your resources of time, money, and heart today. Write a (+) or (-) sign to indicate how positively or negatively you are influencing these people in their walk with God (or towards Him if they are not Christians). Then, using a different colored ink, write down the names of all the individuals who have an impact on you. Write down the specific impact that each one is having ("modeling for me how to be a godly wife," "showing me what it looks like to forgive," etc.). Put a (+) or (-) sign by each one to indicate how negatively or positively he or she is influencing you in your walk with God.

- What does the overall picture look like? Are you being more positively than negatively influenced by others? Are you having a positive impact or negative impact on others?

- What changes do you need to make to the team that surrounds you? Do you need to surround yourself with Christians who are modeling godly living for you?

- What do you need to change to be a better influence for Christ? Do you need to focus your resources on more fertile ground? Do you need to do a better job of talking about the impact that Christ has had on you?

PROGRESS *Not Perfection*

19

STOP COMPETING
AND START
COLLABORATING

I love the Olympics and seeing all those amazing athletes in one place at one time. They are the best of the best in every kind of athletic endeavor, from nations all over the world. What is even more amazing is seeing how each of them has been shaped and formed in a different way, through coaching and training. Though most of them were born with a physical gift for athleticism, it was hard work and training that prepared their bodies to excel in their sport, their minds to be strong and disciplined, and their spirits to be focused. As a result of all this, they have each become the top competitors in their sport.

While I love seeing these athletes at the height of their competition, I wonder what it would look like if we all stopped trying to be better than everyone else and instead started working together to be the best we can be for God. When we stop competing for God's attention and start collaborating to do God's will, we begin to really make a difference for God. It takes a highly focused and disciplined person to excel in his or her own gift. It takes a wise person to value the God-given gifts in others, overlook the weak areas in others, and figure out how to pull out the best in everyone.

NONE OF US CAN ACHIEVE GOD'S PURPOSES ALONE.

Each of us has something to offer and none of us can achieve God's purposes alone. Together we can make the difference. All are needed – the only question is whether each of us is willing to work together to do God's will.

"To one there is given through the Spirit a message of wisdom, to another a message of knowledge by means of the same Spirit, to another faith by the same Spirit, to another gifts

of healing by that one Spirit, to another miraculous powers, to another prophecy, to another distinguishing between spirits, to another speaking in different kinds of tongues, and to still another the interpretation of tongues."
(1 Corinthians 12:8-10)

―――◈―――

STEP TO PROGRESS

Keep this book with you today and write down in it one God-given gift that you see in each of the people you live with or with whom you work closely. When you get home this evening, beside each person's name and gift, write down what all of you can work together to do that will make a difference for the Kingdom of God. Then, tomorrow, go and share this.

_____

_____

_____

_____

_____

PROGRESS *Not Perfection*

20
FAITH COMES OUT FROM WITHIN

How often have you attended a great event and bought the t-shirt, book, CD, or DVD only to go home and put it all on the "memories" shelf? When someone comes to our home, they will see our shelf of memories, packed with amazing events and things we have done (celebrations, concerts, conferences, trips, experiences, vacations, family moments, and more). Though it is fun to share our lives with people we invite into our home, and with whom we choose to have a personal relationship, I think God wants more from us.

God is far more concerned with what happens to us on the inside as a result of memorable events and activities than what is seen on the outside of us. He wants those moments to change us to be more like Him so that we, in turn, will be motivated to go out and help others make changes in their lives.

God acts through people like you and me. He knows that what is seen on the outside of us represents us far less than what is on the inside. He also knows that He can give us a million experiences and we can remain unchanged, especially if those experiences remain passively sitting there on our memory shelf. When we allow those experiences to change us to be like Him, we will put them into practice to help others.

*WHAT IS SEEN...
IS ON THE
INSIDE.*

Find the time to look closely at your shelf of memories. Write down each of the experiences and activities represented there. Then write down how God changed you through each one. Pull out your Bible and use the references to find what God has to say about your experiences.

Don't just buy the book, take a picture, or wear the t-shirt. Dig more deeply into your life, more deeply into the Word, and thank God for what He has done inside you. Then go out into the world and share with others what God has done for you. Pray that God will use you as a light shining in the darkness for everyone you encounter.

"Arise, shine, for your light has come, and the glory of the LORD rises upon you." (Isaiah 60:1)

STEP TO PROGRESS

Go back through your life and identify the moments when your understanding of God deepened, along with your relationship and connection with Him. Write a few sentences about each moment. Be careful to include anyone who helped you in each moment. Take this list and find one Bible verse that contains what God taught you in that moment. After doing this, you will have a list of experiences you are highly qualified to go out and share with others. Use them to encourage people in their time of need.

PROGRESS *Not Perfection*

21
TRUST GOD

I am so thankful that my parents taught me to not put my faith in things. Previous generations were reminded of this during the Great Depression and the economic depression that took place in the 1980s. My generation has been reminded of this during bombings, economic and financial crises, and turmoil in the housing market. During these times, people who previously had much found themselves starting over financially and devastated emotionally. Their security (money, position, status) was stripped out from under them. God used these circumstances to reposition the hearts and perspective of many of His children!

God wants us to trust Him. Putting our trust in money, title, position, economies, or even people is not what He says we are supposed to do. All of those things can disappear in a second – they are not everlasting, all-powerful, or all-knowing. By the same token, if we put our trust in people (a minister, a spouse, a parent, a friend, a leader, and others), we start turning them into our God instead of pointing our faith and trust towards God. Everyone is on their own path of progress and on their own journey. They are equally full of fleshly imperfection! If your faith and trust are in others, you will always be disappointed.

God's Word teaches us to put our faith in Him and Him alone – not in things, and not in people. While material things are something to appreciate and enjoy, they are not to define us or become the basis for our happiness. While God commands us to love people just as He loves us, we are not to put our faith in people. We are to put our faith in Him.

"Do not trust a neighbor; put no confidence in a friend. Even with the woman who lies in your embrace guard the words of your lips. For a son dishonors his father, a daughter rises up against her mother, a daughter-in-law against her mother-in-law – a man's enemies are the

*members of his own household. But as for me, I
watch in hope for the Lord, I wait for God my
Savior; my God will hear me." (Micah 7:5-7)*

STEP TO PROGRESS

Take a look at your life. (Look in every closet.)
If a tornado hit your home tomorrow and wiped it
and all your things away, what would you miss the
most? Losing which items would really devastate
you? Think about the comforts and luxuries, the
pictures and physical things that trigger wonderful
memories. Think about the boxes in closets and
china in cabinets. Consider the family heirlooms.
What would be different for you with all of these
things gone?

Now make a list of everything in your life that
the tornado could not rip away. Examples could be:
my faith, my trust in God, my lifetime of service, my
love for others, my integrity, and so on. Thank God
for these things and put your trust in God to help
you turn your focus on them.

PROGRESS *Not Perfection*

22

SURRENDER AND LET GO

In 2008, our national economy came to a screeching halt when the United States' housing bubble burst. Scores of individuals and families who had known long-term financial security and enjoyed a stable income found themselves in debt and desperate to find a way to make a living. Some lost everything. The national crisis had a personal impact on everyone in our country. Dreams of retirement vanished. Visions of financial security were gone. Their circumstances gave them a forced lesson on what it means to "surrender all."

People who had their security wrapped up in their positions, titles, or even the size of their home(s) or retirement account(s) had to rethink what defined them. Many turned to alcohol, drugs, affairs, divorce, and even suicide to cope with their pain, loss, insecurity, and fear. Thankfully, many others found their answer in their faith – in knowing that God made them to be more than these worldly things of money and title.

For us, the national crisis was further exacerbated by the discovery of an even deeper crisis revealed to us by an auditor who was evaluating our own companies – a decade-long history of lies and theft by one of our own family members. While the thought of the money lost was certainly overwhelming (over 2.2 million dollars plus the costs associated with fixing the problems that were created), our real pain and suffering came out of our realization that someone we loved and trusted had violated us so deeply.

How would you fare if all you had worked so long and hard for was suddenly gone, or if in a single moment you found out the last ten years were defined by a series of repeated lies by people you loved? Where would you turn? What or who would you hold on to for security? Would you stand firm in the truths that you knew from God or hold tight to the dollar amount in your checkbook? Would you be more concerned with what you lost or being sure that the people around you found God in the process? Are you more worried today with how your house (or someone else's house) looks or how your eternal life looks? What will you sacrifice to have more money or to serve God? God calls us to turn it all over to Him, to not want what others have, and to focus our hearts and minds on the more long-term focus of eternal life (not on the immediate focus of what you have today or even the short-term focus of what is in your retirement account). While God does want us to be good stewards, He does not want us to sacrifice our eternal life for these more worldly things. As you begin to make God your focus, you will discover a new place of peace and an everlasting sense of security that no worldly source can bring.

"Trust in the LORD with all your heart and lean not on your own understanding; in all your ways submit to him, and he will make your paths straight." (Proverbs 3:5-6)

—✦—═◯═—✦—

STEP TO PROGRESS

Write down the things that make you feel secure and safe. Perhaps owning your own home is one. Could it be your 401k or retirement savings? Is it your investment portfolio or country club membership? Is it your education or career? Whatever they are, write them down. Now turn all these things over to God in prayer. Give Him control over these things and make a commitment to follow His guidance in all you do with them. This does not necessarily mean you must go out and give these things away to the poor. It does mean you must release the control these things have over your heart, body, and mind to trust in God to meet all your needs.

23
THE WORLD'S WAY IS NOT GOD'S WAY

"Turn the other cheek" is something that Jesus teaches us with His life as it is described by His disciples. When I read the passages that illustrate how He consistently made this choice, I realize how far I have yet to go in following Him! To follow God is to respond the way Christ would respond – not the way the world responds. It is so easy to get caught up in focusing on what other people have taken from you, done to hurt you, or said about you. God's Word clearly says that what others do to you is completely irrelevant – what matters is how you respond.

GOD'S WORD CLEARLY SAYS WHAT OTHERS DO TO YOU IS IRRELEVANT - WHAT MATTERS IS HOW YOU RESPOND.

The late Rev. Billy Joe Daugherty of Victory Christian Center in Tulsa, Oklahoma, offered a live and very public example of how we are to live out this passage from God's Word. Google his name and you will see a video clip depicting a man who came up and struck Rev. Daugherty in the face twice in the middle of an altar call and prayer. Rather than striking back, Rev. Daugherty immediately gathered his congregation in prayer for the man. He even went to visit the man following the incident in an effort to reach his soul. What an incredible leader and example for Christ Rev. Daugherty was as he lived out this passage so powerfully.

The Rev. Daugherty was struck by someone full of anger and hatred. He struck back with God's greatest weapon – love. So often in our business life, we have been faced with decisions of whether to "strike back" when someone strikes us. We have consistently found ourselves in circumstances where we had to choose whether to strike back with equally venomous behavior or to simply follow Christ in defending what is right or protecting innocent people. As an attorney, I have had to wrestle with what exactly the Bible says on these things –

particularly when it comes to being taken into court or choosing to assert claims in court. Sometimes what we feel like doing is not what the Bible says should be done. Thankfully, we have had a wise advocate and advisors around us for two decades who made sure we stayed on course with what we believed and God teaches in these areas.

> *"You have heard that it was said, 'Eye for eye, and tooth for tooth.' But I tell you, do not resist an evil person. If anyone slaps you on the right cheek, turn to them the other cheek also. And if anyone wants to sue you and take your shirt, hand over your coat as well. If anyone forces you to go one mile, go with them two miles. Give to the one who asks you, and do not turn away from the one who wants to borrow from you." (Matthew 5:38-42)*

STEP TO PROGRESS

Identify someone who has "struck out" at you in anger or hatred. How did you respond? Was your knee-jerk reaction to yell? To hit back? To "get in their face"? Or did you respond with Christ's peace, kindness, and love? Write down what you did and how you could have done it better. It is easy to think we have it all figured out until we take a hard look at how we react to attacks from others, or to negative events and circumstances. Make a commitment today to react in a new way – to choose love and peace over striking back with venom, to defending truth and honor rather than justifying wrong behaviors or choices, to accepting unfortunate results and learning through them rather than blaming someone for them.

24

HANG UP ON YOUR "SELF" TO ANSWER GOD'S CALL

I remember being in my early thirties and facing the decision of a lifetime. I was the ultimate over-achieving, career-minded professional – attorney, legal services director for a large healthcare system, board member of several nonprofits, active in my church, training for a 15k run – you name it, I was doing it. Of course, you can guess where my focus was – what can *I* achieve next? (Yes, that was "I.") I was self-driven, self-motivated, and self-accomplished.

Without question, God needed me to realize that I had to surrender my "self" to Him. I quickly found myself deciding between pursuing my corporate law career and becoming a part-time, self-employed stepmom to my new husband's two children. Talk about surrender! I set aside every ounce of what I had been driven to achieve for thirty years to focus my energy on making sure that a total of about five months out of the year, two little boys had everything they needed.

I would love to tell you that this was my one major lesson in surrender. However, it seems that with every new step of faith in my life, I give more of my "self" to God. Each time I think, *I have nothing more to give, God!* Yet, with each new step of faith, I do have more to give – my career, my heart, my time, my money, my passions, my financial security, my desires, my mind, my gifts…and the list keeps going!

With each new part of my "self" that I surrender, I find a new sense that I am fulfilling God's purpose for me and my life. Not once have I thought to myself, *I wish I could take back what I turned over to God.* So, here I am in my mid-forties with three children still in our home and owning and running two of our companies – yet, I am waking up early in the morning, writing about the seeds in my life that have made my journey meaningful and even some of the lessons I have learned the hard way. Why give up my sleep and my mornings for this? Simple. God called me to share my story, so I must constantly hang up on my "self" to answer His call.

"But you are a chosen people, a royal priesthood, a holy nation, God's special possession, that you may declare the praises of him who called you out of darkness into his wonderful light. But if you suffer for doing good and you endure it, this is commendable before God. To this you were called, because Christ suffered for you, leaving you an example, that you should follow in his steps." (1 Peter 2:9, 20-21)

STEP TO PROGRESS

When you look back over your life, what have you given up in order to do what God has called you to do? Are you harboring resentment and anger over giving up those things, or do you realize that you are getting closer to the life God has for you? What are you currently holding on to that God is calling you to give up? How would giving these things up to God empower you to serve Him better?

Write down three things you will do this week to give those things up to God. Turn over to God the extra time, money, and room in your heart.

25
MAKE THE CHOICE

Free will causes us to make choices every day. Some of our choices cause us to rejoice, while others cause us to repent and start over! Every single one of us has made both kinds of choices and lived with both kinds of results. Which of these do you choose to serve each day: God, or something (or someone) else?

I used to get up and exercise at the gym first thing every morning. My workout began at 5:30 or 6:00 a.m. My daily routine ran like a well-oiled machine. I set the alarm for 4:15 a.m.; got up, got dressed, and brushed my teeth by 4:30 a.m.; made coffee and sat down to read my Bible by 4:45 a.m.; walked out the door for my workout by 5:20 a.m. It all ran so smoothly...until one day – one ever so horrible day.

ONE SEEMINGLY SMALL WRONG CHOICE CAN TAKE YOU DOWN A LONG AND WINDING PATH OF MISERY.

On that day, I chose to do some work from the office at 4:45 a.m. instead of reading my Bible. That one choice on one day soon became my new habit for many days until, suddenly, I was no longer doing what God had purposed for my life. For three miserable years, I suffered. I labored without food for my spirit. I was exhausted in my soul and drained in my faith. One seemingly small wrong choice can take you down a long and winding path of misery.

Thankfully, I woke up one day and said, "This has got to stop." I knew I needed a restart and have not looked back since.

I still work at odd hours when God stirs me in the night or early in the morning (as people who work closely with me can readily attest), but I start every day the same way: reading my Bible, surrendering my heart and life, and just being present with God. That choice sets me in a completely different direction – God's direction instead of mine.

Look at how you start each day. You may need a restart too to get your heart, head, and household headed in the right direction with God.

> *"But if serving the LORD seems undesirable to you, then choose for yourselves this day whom you will serve, whether the gods your ancestors served beyond the Euphrates, or the gods of the Amorites, in whose land you are living. But as for me and my household, we will serve the LORD." (Joshua 24:15)*

⊰⊷⊷═◉═⊶⊶⊱

STEP TO PROGRESS

Write down your typical morning routine, including the time you wake up and everything else you do. Where did time with God find a place on your list? If necessary, rewrite your routine so that you actually start each day by spending time with God. Make a commitment to start the next three days in a row by spending time with God. After this, write down how spending time with God made a difference each of those three days.

PROGRESS *Not Perfection*

If you already spend time with God each morning, ask yourself, *What one choice am I making, day after day, that has had the most impact on my ability to live a full, quality life for God?* Are you overcommitted, with a packed schedule? Are you driving your husband and children crazy with activities and goals? If you chose to take one of these activities or commitments away, what would be the positive impact on your quality of life?

26

WHAT YOU LOSE IN THE WORLD IS NOT WHAT MATTERS – IT IS WHAT YOU GAIN FOR GOD

Loss. In many ways, it is the most dreaded of life experiences. Loss of life (death), loss of relationships (divorce), loss of health, loss of security (money and assets), loss of name (reputation or fame) – these are the top causes of stress and strife.

What would happen if we changed our perspective on loss, viewing it as an opportunity rather than something that happens to us? What if we viewed loss not merely as the lopping off of people, possessions, or things from our lives, but as an opportunity for new growth to occur in us?

God wants us to cut back the dead branches in our spiritual lives so that new blooms of growth can come. Loss helps us to do this. While we often do not choose these losses, we can choose to make them starting points for new growth.

The life of Judith Mayotte provides a beautiful example of how loss can become an opportunity for new life and tremendous growth. The woman I grew up knowing as "Aunt Judy," lived a life that was more Christlike than any person I have known. From her work with the Desmond Tutu Peace Foundation in South Africa, to her service with the refugees of war-torn portions of South Africa, she has lived a devoted life of love and service to God.

She gave up her possessions, overcame polio, lost a husband, lost her leg receiving an air shipment of food in a refugee camp, and ultimately had to give up what she loved doing most; all to commit her life to peace and reconciliation. What she has gained for God in the way of planting seeds of love, peace, and service has been far greater than any worldly loss she experienced. With every loss in her life, she saw opportunities to give more.

If you are playing sports on a team, your win-loss record defines your overall team strength. The same holds true in our spiritual lives. For every loss you experience, what are you doing to make room for new growth in your walk with God?

WHAT ARE YOU DOING TO MAKE ROOM FOR NEW GROWTH IN YOUR WALK WITH GOD?

"What good is it for someone to gain the whole world, yet forfeit their soul?" (Mark 8:36)

STEP TO PROGRESS

Write down the three biggest losses you have faced in your lifetime. For each loss, write down what you did (or could have done) in response to each one to create growth in your spiritual life and gain from God. What did God give to you or deliver to you during that time of loss to take you from the desert into the Promised Land? Now thank God for the spiritual growth and gain that resulted from the losses you've experienced.

PROGRESS *Not Perfection*

27

FILL YOUR HEART AND HOME WITH PRAISE

I woke up one morning and looked out my glass front door to see a beautiful sight only a late May day can bring – hydrangeas – beautifully blooming and showering my front walkway with a brilliant fuchsia pink. I could not imagine a more joyful sight. I love hydrangeas – you plant them and they grow year after year – always blooming with more blossoms each time. What I love most is that all I have to do is cut away the dead stems each winter. With a minimum of care, they bring me joy year after year, and prove to be a great way for me to shower others with a little springtime love.

I think this is how God looks at us as we make progress in our lives. God is not nearly as concerned with the times when our blossoms fade and wither, or the large number of dead branches and flowers He has to cut away from our lives – He cares more about how beautifully we bloom after He has cut away our dead parts.

Just think what a wonderful world this would be if we all looked at one another in this way, whether during a dead season or that first spring day. What if all we saw in others was a wonderful flowering plant that would produce beauty and joy, year after year?

THE PROMISE IS WORTH EVERY BIT OF ENDURANCE AND PAIN.

Fill your heart and your home with this perspective of seeking joy and beauty to praise and you will be amazed at the blossoms that will start showing in your life. Yes, you will still have your dead seasons and endure some painful pruning, but the promise of beautiful new blooms is worth every bit of endurance and pain.

"Now learn this lesson from the fig tree: As soon as its twigs get tender and its leaves

come out, you know that summer is near."
(Matthew 24:32)

STEP TO PROGRESS

Identify three times in your life when you bloomed and blossomed most. Write a short sentence about each one.

Look at your life right now.

- What do you see budding in your life that is ready to bloom and blossom?

- Are you growing in your understanding of God? Why do you say this?

- Are you finding new ways to share your faith life and experiences with others who do not yet know God? What are some of them?

- Are you creating new life in others with your words and deeds? How so?

Thank God for these new blooms and for the cutting back He has done to help us grow and blossom.

PROGRESS *Not Perfection*

28
LIVE BY THE GOLDEN RULE

Some days, I return home from work, look around the house and see a million things left out and scattered about, as if the second coming had occurred and my children had just vanished in the middle of doing a host of things. For years, my habit was to say to them (OK, scream at them): "Do you think I am your slave? Pick up your things!"

In hindsight, I was not modeling for them what I had been taught by my mother and was not living the Golden Rule. God's Word gives us a specific, general rule of thumb for our behavior: We should treat others as we would like to be treated.

AM I DOING SOMETHING I WOULD WANT OTHERS TO DO?

So much in our lives would improve if we would ask ourselves every moment of every day, *Am I doing something I would want others to do?* If I throw my trash out the car window for someone else to have to pick up, arrive late to work every day, or ignore someone in need, I am not doing what I would want others to do. Am I treating the city improvement crews, my coworkers and boss, the homeless person starving on the street, and everyone else as I would want to be treated if I were in their shoes? Am I really living out God's Golden Rule?

We all have room to improve. Ask God to show you today what you need to do to live your life more in accordance with the Golden Rule. He may show you that you need to start showing up to work on time to keep people from having to wait for you. It may be to slow down and listen to your child who is desperately trying to get you to give them attention. It may be that you need to spend an evening with your husband or wife, just telling him or her what a wonderful addition they are to your life.

Stop what you are doing. Think about how you behave. Recall the words that have recently come from your mouth. What changes do you need to make? As you live out the Golden Rule more faithfully, you will find a renewed sense of purpose and the peace that God wants for you in your heart, soul, and mind.

"Treat others as you want them to treat you."
(Matthew 7:12 CEV)

STEP TO PROGRESS

Stop, look, and listen to yourself today. Write down three things you do or say that clearly do not adhere to the Golden Rule. Now go to anyone who has been negatively affected by your failure to follow the Golden Rule. Tell them that you would not want them to treat you the way you had treated them, and apologize.

Tomorrow, write down three things that you do or say that are examples of how you do follow the Golden Rule. Write down what it feels like to treat other people the way you want to be treated.

PROGRESS *Not Perfection*

29
WE ARE ALL IN THIS TOGETHER!

How many times have you heard someone say in disgust, "You Christians all think you are better than everyone else!" When I hear this, I want to scream from the mountaintops! Christians are not better than anyone. Every single one of us is in the same boat – we are desperate sinners! We are in a constant battle to set aside our own selfish ways, our own lies and deceptions, and our own filthy pasts. If any of us looks at someone else and thinks, *I am better than that,* then we are missing the truth of God's Word from the outset.

IF ANY OF US LOOKS AT SOMEONE AND THINKS, I AM BETTER, WE ARE MISSING THE TRUTH OF GOD'S WORD.

For me, being a Christian is about my response to the truth we are all in the same boat. The difference is, I have decided to admit I am a pitiful sinner, but am committed to living out God's purpose for my life. This means I eliminate as much sin from my body, mind, and spirit as I can!

In my mind, being a Christian means I am simply focused on a different life vision – God's vision for my life as it was revealed to me in and through the life of Jesus. It means that I am constantly focused on looking at life from a different perspective – an eternal perspective instead of a worldly perspective. It means I am intent on living *in* this world (I shop, eat, relax, work, sleep), but not living as if I am *of* this world. I try not to define myself based on what the world values, but rather on what God values. It means that I try to live out my life with a different goal – to accomplish God's purposes for this world rather than my own.

Of course, this does not mean I always get it right and never head off in the wrong direction. It also does not mean that I will never hurt someone else, or that I will always do only what God wants.

In fact, what it really means is that I am destined to mess up! I will have to go back and clean up the messes I make, over and over again. Hopefully, I will not keep going around the same mountain over and over again (like the Israelites did for forty years), and will just keep moving forward, making progress step-by-step.

If you feel the "Christian" way of life is hypocritical or too high of a standard for you, I urge you to revisit what it really means to be a Christian. If you are a Christian but you find yourself constantly judging the people around you, then I urge you to get back to the Word to remember who you are in Christ – no worse or better than anybody else. We are simply all in the same boat together. Let's start rowing and enjoy the adventure.

> *"So where does that put us? Do we Jews get a better break than the others? Not really. Basically, all of us, whether insiders or outsiders, start out in identical conditions, which is to say that we all start out as sinners. Scripture leaves no doubt about it: There's nobody living right, not even one, nobody who knows the score,*

nobody alert for God. They've all taken the wrong turn; they've all wandered down blind alleys. No one's living right; I can't find a single one…And it's clear enough, isn't it, that we're sinners, every one of us, in the same sinking boat with everybody else? Our involvement with God's revelation doesn't put us right with God. What it does is force us to face our complicity in everyone else's sin." (Romans 3:9-12,19-20 MSG)

STEP TO PROGRESS

- What are some ways to intentionally reveal to people around you that you are a Christian, but weak, imperfect, and very much a work in progress?

- How can you stop trying to "look" like you are living a model life (all while you are hiding your imperfections or denying them) and instead talk openly about where you have it all wrong and are working to live a better life for God?

- How would openly discussing your failures and shortcomings along with the good, change the way non-Christians perceive you as a Christian? What would the impact of this be on fellow Christians? What characteristic of Christ will you be showing by doing this?

PROGRESS *Not Perfection*

30

SEEK GODLY NOT "GIRLY" COUNSEL

So many women look for advice from women's magazines, business journals, coworkers, neighbors, family members, or friends. Where do you turn for advice and sound counsel? How many of these people and sources advise you based on a worldly viewpoint rather than from a foundation in the Word of God?

I can't tell you how many times I have turned to people for advice who were living just as messed up a life as I was. Why exactly I thought they could help me, I do not know. What I do know now is that when we need advice and counsel, we must turn to people and sources that base what they say on God's Word.

This may sound funny coming from a licensed attorney of nearly twenty years who has predicated

her education and life on giving sound risk manage-
ment advice, but the wisest counsel you can seek is
God's counsel. This does not mean you should not
go to others to gather facts or evaluate situations,
but when it comes down to making a final decision,
seek God's wisdom for your life. Once I see clearly
the truth and extent of my situation or challenge –

GOD'S WISDOM
IS REVEALED
WHEN WE ARE
WILLING TO SEE
OUR SITUATION
FROM GOD'S
PERSPECTIVE.

all the good, the bad, and the
ugly – I can open up my Bible
and seek God's wisdom. God's
wisdom is revealed when we
open our hearts up to listen for
God's wisdom and are willing to
see our situation clearly from
God's perspective.

When I dig into God's Word,
I hear clearly and know the path I
must follow. I might not like
what I read or what I hear (that sinful nature keeps
getting in the way), but ultimately the Bible gives
me the best advice on how to live my life (or how
NOT to live my life, as the case may be). In the end,
I receive God's strength to see me through every
situation I face.

As you go about your day today, be mindful of the counsel and advice you seek from other people. Practice seeking God's Word first, then gathering facts and godly wisdom, and finally, submitting yourself to God so you can see His perspective.

"If you accept my words and store up my commands within you, turning your ear to wisdom and applying your heart to understanding – indeed, if you call out for insight and cry aloud for understanding, and if you look for it as for silver and search for it as for hidden treasure, then you will understand the fear of the Lord and find the knowledge of God. For the Lord gives wisdom and from his mouth come knowledge and understanding…Then you will understand what is right and just and fair – every good path. For wisdom will enter your heart, and knowledge will be pleasant to your soul." (Proverbs 2:1-6,9-10)

STEP TO PROGRESS

Look back over the past week of your life and identify the three top sources of advice you sought.

Was it your best friend? Parent? Spouse? Coworker? Did you read a women's magazine to find the latest fashions or newest trends for your life? Are you willing to stop seeking these sources for what to do in your life to ask God instead?

If you are, then start each day this week with this prayer: Dear God, You are my Maker and my Creator; You are the beginning and the end – all powerful, all knowing, and all understanding. You see my path before I myself see it or take it. God, I ask today that You reveal to me the direction I should take in this situation [name the situation]. As I look to Your Word, reveal to me what You alone know I need to hear. Show me, teach me, mold me, make me, oh Lord, and I will follow You first and always. Amen.

31
FORGIVENESS IS A ONE-WAY STREET

It is hard to believe that I was nearly halfway through my life before I fully understood the difference between forgiveness and reconciliation, but it is true. I always understood that forgiveness was a choice I was to make – a loving choice I made because I had been forgiven, in spite of my weaknesses and failures. I also knew that forgiving myself for my own failures was essential to being able to forgive others.

Somehow, I confused my choice to forgive with God's will for me to be reconciled with those I had forgiven. I believed that God's command to love others demanded that I be reconciled with someone who had yet to seek reconciliation with me. But forgiving another person requires me only to make a unilateral choice. The other person has to do absolutely nothing in order for me to choose to forgive them.

The truth is that God's idea of true peace between people cannot be found until the forgiveness comes full circle and reconciliation takes place – I forgive myself, I forgive the other person, the other person forgives himself or herself, and then forgives me.

TRUE PEACE BETWEEN PEOPLE CANNOT BE FOUND UNTIL FORGIVENESS COMES FULL CIRCLE.

So often we unilaterally forgive another, but one or more steps of the circle of forgiveness is broken. As a result, true peace and reconciliation are not found. What God's Word teaches us is that we can only be held accountable for our part – for the acts of forgiving ourselves and the other person. From there, we must wait on the other person to forgive themselves, and then to forgive us.

So what do you do when you are in a relationship with someone who is not willing to complete the circle of reconciliation? Pull back and pray for them. Pray for them to heal, to forgive themselves and, in turn, to forgive you. Pray that they find peace through the Word of God. Then choose to think loving thoughts, speak loving words, and pray blessings over their life…but do these things from afar so that they cannot continue to hurt you or steal joy from you. Do not let their hard heart keep you from achieving all that God has for you.

In this way, you will live out God's greatest command…

> *"You have heard that it was said 'Love your neighbor and hate your enemy.' But I tell you, love your enemies and pray for those who perse-cute you, that you may be children of your Father in heaven. He causes his sun to rise on the evil and the good, and sends rain on the righteous and the unrighteous." (Matthew 5:43-45)*

STEP TO PROGRESS

Identify one relationship you have (or had) with someone in which the circle of forgiveness is not complete (at least on their part), and reconciliation and peace have not been found. Say a prayer over that person's life and speak words of blessing toward him or her. Keep praying throughout the day for this person – regardless of the pain they may have caused you, regardless of whether they have as yet acknowledged what they have done. God will bless you with peace in your heart and abundant life in the process.

Now identify a relationship you have which illustrates the full circle of forgiveness; where peace and reconciliation have been found. Say a prayer of thanks and praise God for accomplishing His will in that relationship. Reach out to this person and thank him or her for being willing to choose love and overcome the obstacles with you. Honor him or her today.

LIVING A LIFE OF PROGRESS NOT PERFECTION

It is my prayer that you will read these daily truths prayerfully, take time to evaluate your life, surrender yourself to God, and apply God's Word to your life. As you do, I am confident that you will take steps of progress and find your life transformed. With your own transformation, you can then become the catalyst for transforming the lives of others.

These thirty-one Steps to Progress you have worked through can be used at any stage of life. Real truths last a lifetime and across generations. From time to time, when you find yourself stuck in the rut of daily living, find that joy and peace again by rereading these truths and acting on the Step to Progress life application in each one.

Remember, transformation will (and must) take place in your life daily, but will come about over time. You will always be better than you were before, but will always have a long way to go. Find peace in this process. Teach others what you have already overcome, turning your own transformation into your testimony. Learn from others who have gone where you have not yet dared to go. When you live this life of ongoing transformation, you will know that you are fulfilling the purpose God has for you.

Truth4transformation is committed to delivering information that helps transform lives. Proceeds from each book purchased will go to help not-for-profit organizations deliver life-changing information, education, personal support, and opportunities to individuals in crisis, despair, or need. Visit www.nancyrobertslive.com to find out more about the organizations we currently drive which give us the opportunity to help others.

ABOUT THE AUTHOR

Nancy Lynn Roberts is a Christian woman, wife, mother, stepmother, daughter, sister, and business owner who has overcome great challenges, but never stopped looking to God's Word to make progress in her everyday life. She and her husband, Dan, have owned and operated companies together since they married in 1998.

A native Oklahoman, Mrs. Roberts graduated from Pomona College of the Claremont Colleges and subsequently obtained her law degree at the University of Oklahoma, College of Law. After working as an attorney with a corporate law firm in private practice, she took her law degree out into the business world where she met her husband, a former minister turned entrepreneur.

Together, they have relied on their faith and the hope God has put inside them to navigate the challenges brought about by running companies, raising children, and living out their faith.

NEXT IN THE
TRUTH4TRANSFORMATION
SERIES

This book was created based on the everyday life truths that the author has learned and her desire to share these truths with others in the hope that their lives may be transformed. The lessons were written in the order in which they were learned during the life of the author. More truths to come, including ways to transform your workplace, home, and marriage.

For more information, to purchase books,
or to schedule Nancy Lynn Roberts to speak,

please visit the author at
www.nancyrobertslive.com.

NOTES

NOTES

NOTES